Soccer Sense

Terms, Tips & Techniques

Paul S. Delson

Excalibur Press
4 Chestnut Street
San Carlos, CA 94070

ACKNOWLEDGEMENTS

The author wishes to extend his deepest appreciation to the following people, without whose help this book would never have been created and published:

NEIL POSNER and DEL DELSON, for their editing assistance;

MICHAEL McGOVERN, for his cartoons;

DOUG WINN, for his photographs;

DONN DELSON, for his publishing assistance;

CHRIS LINNETT, for his cover design, diagrams and publishing assistance; and

DOUG OAKES, for his soccer wisdom.

The author would also like to thank his parents and brothers for their advice, support and love.

Library of Congress Catalog Card Number: 93-90052

Copyright © 1993 by Paul S. Delson

ISBN 0-9634669-0-9

Published by Excalibur Press

Printed in the United States of America

PREFACE

SOCCER SENSE: TERMS, TIPS & TECHNIQUES is a reference guide for soccer players of all ages and abilities, their parents and all others interested in learning more about the world's most popular sport.

The primary purpose of this book is to define, in simple terms, those words and phrases most frequently used in playing and coaching the game of soccer. The secondary purpose of this book is to provide tips and techniques for the player and/or coach so that the definitions are given additional meaning within the context of the soccer game. The tips and techniques are set apart from the definition by a ⚽.

I applaud the fact that soccer is a game which is enjoyed by both males and females. In writing this book, I have tried to avoid gender-specific terms. In those cases where such terms cannot be avoided, I have alternated between the uses of "he/his" and "she/her".

ADVANTAGE RULE

A rule which allows the referee to continue play after a foul occurs if the referee believes that stopping play would give an advantage to the team that caused the foul. For example: a fullback on one team trips a wing on the other team who has the ball, but the wing keeps both her balance and control of the ball. At this point, the referee must decide whether to call a tripping foul and stop play or let play continue under the advantage rule.

⚽ If you make a foul or have a foul made against you, keep playing until you hear the referee's whistle. The referee may have used the advantage rule to let play continue. (See PLAY ON.)

APSL - AMERICAN PROFESSIONAL SOCCER LEAGUE

A professional outdoor soccer league in the United States which was formed in 1990 with the merger of the Western Soccer League and the American Soccer League.

AYSO - AMERICAN YOUTH SOCCER ORGANIZATION

Founded in 1964, this organization promotes youth soccer in the United States.

BACKHEADING

A way to head the ball when a player is facing away from the direction in which the player wants the ball to go. This keeps the ball going in the same general direction it was going when it came to the player. A backheader may be used to shoot on goal or to pass the ball.

⚽ It is important to make contact with the ball at a spot higher on your head than where you would normally head the ball. (See Photos 1 and 2.) Depending on how the ball comes to you, the best spot may vary from the top of your forehead all the way to the back of your head. (See HEADING.)

Photo 1   Photo 2

BACKHEEL

A short distance pass made with the back of the foot which allows the player who passes the ball to move in the opposite direction from the pass.

⚽There are two ways to backheel: (1) by kicking your foot straight back (see Photos 3 and 4), or (2) by crossing your kicking leg in front of your other leg and then kicking back. Before you make a backheel, you should be sure that you have a teammate in back of you who is open for the pass.

Photo 3   Photo 4

BACK PASS

A pass made in the direction of a player's own goal. On offense, a forward might pass back to a halfback to pull a player on the other team towards the ball and out of position. The forward would then be open for a return pass from the halfback. On defense, a fullback with the ball, but with no room to dribble or pass to a halfback, could pass the ball back to the goalie.

⚽Talking to your teammates is important. If you have the ball, you should let your teammates know that you are going to make a pass. If you are behind a teammate who has the ball, you should tell your teammate that you are open for a back pass. When you want to make a back pass to the goalie, pass the ball to the side of the goal and not right at the goal. This is done in case the goalie misses the ball or the ball goes to a player on the other team.

BALL CONTROL

The ability to trap, kick, pass and dribble the ball. A player has a "feel for the ball" or a "good touch" when it becomes easy to play the ball with the feet, head and body.

⚽The ability to control the ball is the key to soccer. Juggling is a good way to improve ball control. Other tips: (1) practice barefoot (on grass only) to learn where your foot should hit the ball; (2) watch the ball as you juggle or kick; (3) practice with a small ball to improve your skills; and (4) learn to trap, kick, pass and dribble the ball with both feet. (See DRIBBLING, JUGGLING, KICKING, PASSING and TRAPPING.)

BALL PERSON

A person who retrieves the ball when it goes out of bounds. The ball person carries an extra ball so that the game may continue while the ball person retrieves the ball which went out of bounds. There are usually at least two ball persons per field. (See OUT OF BOUNDS.)

BANANA KICK

A kick used to make the ball curve. A banana kick is used to pass the ball around players or to shoot on goal. If kicked with the inside of the right foot (or the outside of the left foot), the ball will curve to the left. The ball will curve to the right when hit with the outside of the right foot (or the inside of the left foot).

⚽To curve the ball, kick it slightly off-center on the side away from the way you want it to curve. (See INSWINGER and OUTSWINGER.)

BICYCLE KICK

(See OVERHEAD VOLLEY.)

BREAKAWAY

When the offensive team makes a quick attack towards the goal with more players than the defensive team, such as when three forwards attack against two fullbacks. Another example is when an offensive player with the ball gets past the last defensive player and goes one-on-one against the goalie. A breakaway usually happens because of excellent hustle and teamwork by the offense or because the defense makes a mistake in passing the ball or marking the offensive players.

⚽If you are defending against a breakaway, you should try to slow down the attack so that your teammates have time to get back on defense. The goalie must be alert and in position to stop a shot on goal. If you are on offense, you should spread the attack to make it harder for the other team to mark the offensive players. If you are the player with the ball, you may try to lure a defender onto you and then pass the ball, or you may fake a pass, dribble past the defender and take a shot on goal. (See CONTAINMENT, FEINTING, MARKING, NARROWING THE ANGLE and ONE-ON-ONE.)

"CARRY"

A call to a teammate with the ball to tell her that she is not being marked by a player on the other team and is free to dribble.

CAUTION

(See WARNING.)

CENTER

Players on the forward, halfback and fullback lines who play in the middle of the field when viewed from their own goal. (See FORWARD, FULLBACK and HALFBACK.)

CENTER CIRCLE

A circle on the midfield line from where kickoffs are taken. The circle has a 10 yard radius. (See FIELD, KICKOFF and MIDFIELD LINE.)

CENTER PASS

An offensive pass made from near the sidelines or endline to a teammate who is near or inside the penalty area.

⚽ This pass is usually put in the air to lower the risk of interception. The player who receives the pass can head the ball or trap it and shoot on goal.

CHALLENGE

To try to take the ball away from an opponent. (See TACKLING.)

CHARGE

When a player on one team bumps into a player on the other team, who has the ball, in order to steal the ball. There are four types of charges - three of which are fouls because the bump is too rough for normal play. (1) A "Fair Charge" or "Legal Charge" is when the defensive player, with his arms at his sides, uses his shoulder closest to the player on the other team to make contact with the other player and both players are near the ball. Both players must have at least one foot on the ground when contact is made. This type of charge is not a foul. (2) A "Violent Charge" is a foul where the defensive player makes contact with a player on the other team in a dangerous way. The penalty for this foul is a direct free kick. (3) An "Illegal Charge" is a foul where the defensive player makes too much contact with the player on the other team, although the contact is not violent. This foul usually occurs when the defensive player uses her arms to push the player with the ball or when the defensive player does not have at least

11

one foot on the ground when contact is made. The penalty for this foul is an indirect free kick. (4) "Charging the Goalkeeper" is a foul where an offensive player makes contact with a goalie who has the ball. The penalty for this foul is a direct free kick. (See DIRECT FREE KICK and INDIRECT FREE KICK.)

CHARGING THE GOALKEEPER

(See CHARGE.)

"CHECK"

A call to a teammate with the ball to let him know that a player from the other team is going to try to take the ball away.

Photo 5

Photo 6

CHEST TRAP

When the chest is used to receive and control a ball coming toward a player at chest height.

⚽If the ball is above your head and dropping to you, lean back slightly and pretend that your chest is a table. When the ball makes contact, relax and let your chest travel with the ball to lessen the bounce. It may help you to exhale when the ball makes contact. (See Photo 5.) The ball will bounce and fall to the ground where it can be volleyed or trapped with the sole of your foot. If the ball is coming at you at chest height, lean over it and direct it down to your feet. (See Photo 6.) In both cases, be sure to keep your arms back or out to the side so that you are not called for a hand ball.

CHIP

A short range kick which lifts the ball into the air. A chip usually goes about ten feet high and is used to pass over the head of a player on the other team or to shoot the ball over a goalie who is away from the goal.

⚽This is not a powerful kick. It is used to pass to a teammate who is close by. A chip can also be an effective close range shot on goal if the goalie comes out from the goal. Do not swing your foot forward with much force. The sole of your foot should be parallel to the ground and the ball should be struck from underneath to lift it into the air.

CISL - CONTINENTAL INDOOR SOCCER LEAGUE

A professional indoor soccer league in the United States which began play in 1993.

CLEAR

When the defense moves the ball out of the scoring range of the offense. A clear is made when a defender kicks the ball up the field or out of bounds or when a goalie throws or punts the ball.

⚽Since the clear can be the start of a team's offense, it works best when it is directed to a teammate. If you have the ball but you cannot make a pass, or if you want to clear the ball but you are closely guarded by a player on the other team, you should follow the rule, "When in Doubt, Kick Out". For example, if you are in front of your goal, it is better to kick the ball towards the sideline than it is to try to make, but fail to make, a pass up the field. Kicking the ball towards the sideline or out of bounds will give the rest of your teammates time to get into proper defensive positions.

CONCACAF

The North and Central American and Caribbean Soccer Confederation. Founded in 1961, this organization unites the national soccer associations of twenty-seven North American, Central American and Caribbean countries.

CONMEBOL

The South American Soccer Confederation. Founded in 1916, this is an association of the national soccer associations of ten South American countries.

CONTAINMENT

When a defensive player slows down the speed of attack of a player on the other team who has the ball in order to give the teammates of the defensive player time to get back into good defensive positions.

"Containment"

⚽ If you are on defense, you contain an offensive player with the ball by positioning yourself between the ball and your goal and moving slowly backwards. If you face two opponents, stay closer to the player with the ball but try to stay between the two players so that you can mark the player without the ball if a pass is made to that player. Remember that you cannot go all the way back into your own goal. At some point, usually the eighteen-yard line, you must challenge the offensive player for the ball. (See EIGHTEEN and MARKING.)

COPA LIBERTADORES

The professional club championship of CONMEBOL. Patterned after the European Cup championship, the competition began in 1960 under the name of the Champion Clubs Cup. It received its present name in 1966.

CORNER AREA

The quarter circle area located at each of the four corners of the field from where corner kicks are taken. The circle has a radius of 1 yard. (See CORNER KICK.)

CORNER FLAG

A flag placed at each corner of the field where the endlines and sidelines meet. Soccer rules require that the flags must not be less than 5 feet (1.5 meters) high.

CORNER KICK

A direct free kick given to the offensive team after the ball has gone out of bounds over the endline and was last touched by a player on the defensive team. The kick is taken from the corner area closest to where the ball went out of bounds.

If you are on offense, you should move, before or at the same time the ball is kicked, to a position where you will be open to receive the kick. If you are the player who will kick the ball, you should kick the ball to an area about eight yards out from the goal. This is out of the goalie's reach. You should also look for teammates at the far side of the goal or near the eighteen-yard line. You should move into position on the field after you make the kick. If you are on defense, you should mark players on the other team. The goalie should be positioned at the far side of the goal and a fullback should be at, and slightly inside, the near post. (See CORNER AREA, DIRECT FREE KICK, ENDLINE and NEAR POST.)

COVER

1. To fill a position which has been left open by a teammate who has moved to another position on the field.

2. To mark or guard an opponent.

⚽Tip for definition #1: If you leave your position, you should make sure that a teammate can cover your position if necessary. (See MARKING.)

CROSS

(See CROSSFIELD PASS.)

CROSSBAR

A bar which, when connected to the tops of two goal posts, forms the top of the goal. The width and depth of a crossbar shall not be greater than 5 inches. As a result, crossbars are usually about 24 feet, 10 inches long so that the width of the goal, when measured from the inside of each goal post, is 24 yards. The lower edge of the crossbar must be 8 feet from the ground. The crossbar may be made of metal or wood and the face of the crossbar may be flat or rounded. (See GOAL and GOAL POST.)

CROSSFIELD PASS

A pass made from one side of the field to the other side. This pass is used to change the direction of attack.

⚽This pass can be very effective in building an attack - especially when the other team tends to drop out of position and follow the ball, leaving players on your team open for a pass. A crossfield pass can be straight across the field, such as when a left halfback passes to a right halfback. The pass may also go forward, such as when a left halfback passes to a right wing. If you are on your defensive half of the field, take extra care not to make a bad pass because a bad pass could be intercepted at a point from which the other team could score. To avoid interception, and because of the distance such passes may travel, a crossfield pass should be in the air.

DANGEROUS PLAY

A foul called when a player acts in a way which could be harmful or cause injury to a player on the other team. Examples include: (1) raising a foot, usually near shoulder height, when near a player on the other team; (2) bicycle kicking within six feet of a player on the other team; and (3) lowering one's head to head a ball which is at or lower than waist height when a player on the other team is nearby. The penalty for this foul is an indirect free kick. (See BICYCLE KICK and INDIRECT FREE KICK.)

"Dangerous Play"

DEAD BALL

A ball that is not in play. A ball is a dead ball when: (1) the ball is stopped after the referee calls a foul; (2) the referee calls a time out; (3) the ball has gone out of bounds, resulting in a corner kick, goal kick or throw-in; and (4) a goal has been scored. In all four cases, the ball remains dead until play is restarted with a free kick, throw-in or drop ball.

 Whenever play stops, be alert to when and how the ball will be put back into play. If you are on offense and you have the ball, you should look to pass to a teammate. Your teammates should move to be open to receive a pass. If you are on defense, you should quickly mark an opponent or be in a good defensive position. (See CORNER KICK, DROP BALL, FOUL, FREE KICK, GOAL KICK, OUT OF BOUNDS and THROW-IN.)

"Dead Ball"

DEFENSE

1. When a team or player without the ball tries to stop the team with the ball from scoring a goal.

2. The "defensive" half of the soccer field is the half of the field where a team has its own goal. (See OFFENSE.)

DIRECT FREE KICK

A free kick from which a goal can be scored without any other player touching the ball. A direct free kick is given to a team after the other team has made one of the fouls listed in DIRECT FREE KICK FOULS. A corner kick and a penalty kick are also direct free kicks.

⚽On defense, the players should set up a wall if the kick is taken near the goal. On offense, the player who will kick the ball can either shoot on goal or pass to teammates who should be moving into positions to receive a pass. (See CORNER KICK, DIRECT FREE KICK FOULS, FREE KICK, PENALTY KICK and WALL.)

DIRECT FREE KICK FOULS

A direct free kick is awarded for fouls such as: (1) hand ball; (2) holding; (3) pushing; (4) striking or trying to strike a player on the other team; (5) jumping in; (6) kicking or trying to kick a player on the other team; (7) tripping; (8) charging the goalkeeper when the goalkeeper has the ball; and (9) violent charging.

DISTRIBUTION

When the goalie puts the ball back into play after the goalie has made a save or after the goalie has received the ball from a teammate. The goalie can punt, drop kick, throw or roll the ball into play.

⚽Because distribution is the start of the team's offense, the goalie should try to pass the ball to a teammate instead of simply kicking the ball up the field with the hope that a teammate will receive the ball. A punt is the best way to send the ball far up the field, but a punt is not as accurate as rolling or throwing the ball to a teammate. (See DROP KICK, PUNTING and SAVE.)

DIVE

When a goalie jumps sideways to try to stop a shot on goal from scoring when the shot is not within easy reach. The goalie may try to catch the ball or punch it away.

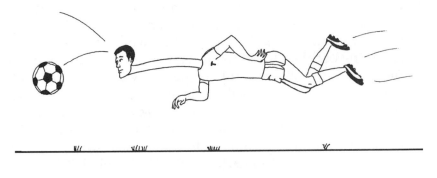You should first practice diving without the ball in order to learn how to land. Begin by diving onto a mattress and then move to the grass as you improve. Also, begin by diving from a crouch (knee height), and work up to a standing position. Always land on your side and keep your eyes on the ball. When you land on the ground, roll so that your back is toward any oncoming players. This protects both you and the ball. (See PUNCHING and SAVE.)

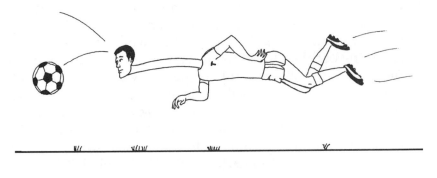

"Diving Header"

DIVING HEADER

Diving to head a ball which is out of reach and usually lower than shoulder level. Offensive players can make diving headers to change low centering passes into shots on goal. Defensive players can make diving headers to clear low passes and shots.

It is best to learn to make a diving header in stages. First, kneel and have a friend throw balls to your head. Dive forward to head the ball. Next, stand up and practice diving. Finally, practice running and diving. In all cases, keep your eyes on the ball and land on the ground with your arms out to your sides, with elbows bent, and your palms down. Practice this only with proper supervision. (See HEADING.)

DRIBBLING

Using the feet to move the ball along the ground. Dribbling may be done while walking or running.

A good dribbler will keep the ball under control. When you are dribbling, keep the ball within a yard of your feet at all times. The closer you are to a player on the other team, the closer you should keep the ball to you. When you are close to an opponent, shield the ball by dribbling with the foot farthest from the opponent. Use feints to dribble past an opponent. When learning to dribble, keep your eyes on the ball and practice with both feet. Try dribbling barefoot to get the feel for where your foot should meet the ball. When you become really good at this skill, you will not have to look directly at the ball as you dribble. Instead, you can use your eyes to look around the field to see where you can dribble or pass the ball. During the game, teammates should tell the player with the ball whether to pass or dribble. (See FEINTING and SHIELDING.)

DROP BALL

A way to put a dead ball back into play where the referee drops the ball between a player from each team. The players cannot kick the ball until it hits the ground. If the ball is kicked before it hits the ground, the referee will stop the game and make another drop ball. Drop balls are used when there are conflicting calls by the referees in a dual referee system. Drop balls are also used to restart play if there is an injury or other type of referee time-out. A goal cannot be scored directly from a drop ball.

If you take a drop ball, you do not have to kick the ball hard. All you have to do is kick the ball to a teammate.

22

Watch the ball. Do not watch the referee or your opponent. Your teammates should be spaced around you in good offensive and defensive positions. (See DEAD BALL, DUAL SYSTEM and TIME-OUT.)

DROP KICK

A way a goalie kicks the ball by dropping the ball and kicking it after it has bounced off the ground.

⚽ You should kick the ball just after it hits the ground. (See DISTRIBUTION.)

DUAL SYSTEM

A system where two referees supervise the game. Each referee is responsible for certain areas of the field, but has equal authority anywhere on the field. This system has not been officially approved by FIFA although it is generally used in college and high school games. (See LINESPERSON, REFEREE and THREE-PERSON SYSTEM.)

DUMMY

(See SELLING A DUMMY.)

DURATION OF THE GAME

The length of time for a non-overtime game. College and professional outdoor games are 90 minutes long (with two 45-minute halves). High school and lower level games range from 60 to 90 minutes. Many youth leagues play four quarters instead of two halves. Indoor soccer games are usually 60 minutes long. (See OVERTIME.)

EIGHTEEN

The eighteen-yard line. This line is 44 yards long, is 18 yards up the field from the endline and forms the top of the penalty area.

⚽ On offense, when the ball is in the corner of the field, a centering pass to this area can be a good offensive play because halfbacks or forwards are often left unguarded at the eighteen. The eighteen is also important on defense because it is a signal to the defensive players that they are near their own goal and must make a play for the ball. (See ENDLINE, FIELD and PENALTY AREA.)

EJECTION

When the referee orders a player to leave the game. This may follow a player's continued breaking of the rules after the player has received a warning. An ejection may also occur without any prior warning, such as when a player starts a fight or tries to hurt another player. An ejected player cannot be replaced. His team must play with one less player than the other team. Play is restarted with a free kick or drop ball. To signal an ejection, the referee holds up a red card.

⚽ If you are ejected from a game, it is best for you and your team if you leave the field quickly and quietly. Remember that the referee is in charge of the game and your team will be playing under the referee's authority. Any further problems which you cause will only hurt your team. (See DROP BALL, FREE KICK, RED CARD and WARNING.)

ENDLINES

The boundary lines which mark the end of the field where each goal is located. The length of the endline is the same as the width of the field. FIFA sets a minimum field width of 50 yards and a maximum field width of 100 yards.

College rules set the width between 65 and 75 yards. (See FIELD.)

EQUIPMENT

Things which are needed to play soccer. These include two goals with nets, corner flags and a soccer ball. A player will wear a jersey, shorts, socks, soccer shoes, shinguards and supporter or sport bra (as needed). Soccer shoes are usually made of leather with rubber or plastic studs on the soles. Gloves may be helpful to a goalie if the ball is wet. Also, the goalie's jersey must be a different color from jerseys worn by the other players and the referee.

EUROPEAN CUP

The championship tournament among the professional soccer club champions from each country in Europe. The competition takes place every year and was first played in 1955.

EXERCISE

Activity which helps a person to become physically fit and, indirectly, mentally fit.

To be good at soccer, you must be physically fit. The more "in shape" your body is, the easier it is to improve your performance and avoid injury. Strength, speed and flexibility are all important - although you do not need huge muscles to be a good soccer player. There are many exercises which will help you to develop certain parts of your body. For example: push-ups can help to make your upper body strong; sit-ups can strengthen your stomach muscles; and running will help you develop speed and endurance. Exercise can be fun. Try exercising with a friend or combine exercise with a soccer drill, such as running with the ball. Vary the exercises so that you do not become bored and be sure to do stretching exercises along with those exercises which build strength. (See PRACTICE and WARMUP.)

FA CUP

The championship tournament for the teams of the First Division soccer leagues in Great Britain. The English FA Cup began in 1870. The Scottish FA Cup started in 1873. The Welsh FA Cup was first played in 1877 and the Irish FA Cup began in 1880.

FAIR CHARGE

(See CHARGE.)

FAKING

(See FEINTING.)

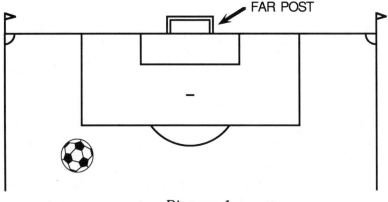

Diagram 1

FAR POST

The goal post which is farthest from the ball. (See Diagram 1.)

The far post is important for both the offense and the defense. On offense, a shot to the far post (or a crossfield pass to a teammate near the far post) has a good chance to score because the goalie will play closer to the near post. On defense, the far post should be covered on corner kicks. A fullback or halfback usually covers the far post, but many goalies like to position themselves at the far post and then move up to the near post if the ball is not kicked far. The goalie must be aware of any players on the other team who could receive a pass at the far post. (See CORNER KICK, CROSSFIELD PASS, GOAL POST and NEAR POST.)

FEINTING

To fool a player on the other team. This can happen when a player with the ball changes running speed or direction to get past a player on the other team, or when an offensive player without the ball changes running speed or direction to lead a player on the other team away from an area or position. The main idea is to make the player on the other team think that the offensive player will move or pass one way when the offensive player is really going to move or pass another way.

⚽If you are on offense, be relaxed. Try to develop quick starts as the first few steps that you take are the ones which can beat your opponent. Quick turns, stepping over the ball, stops and starts and moving the ball between your opponent's legs (nutmeg) are a few of the many feints you can practice. If you are on defense, watch the ball and ignore the foot movements of the player with the ball. Challenge the player for the ball when it is farthest away from the player's feet. (See NUTMEG.)

FIELD

The place where the game of soccer is played. (See Diagram 2.) The playing surface may be grass, dirt or artificial turf. The field should be in the shape of a rectangle. FIFA rules state that the length of the field should be 100 to 130 yards and the width should be 50 to 100 yards. NCAA rules allow a length of 110 to 120 yards and a width of 65 to 75 yards. Certain areas of the field are marked by

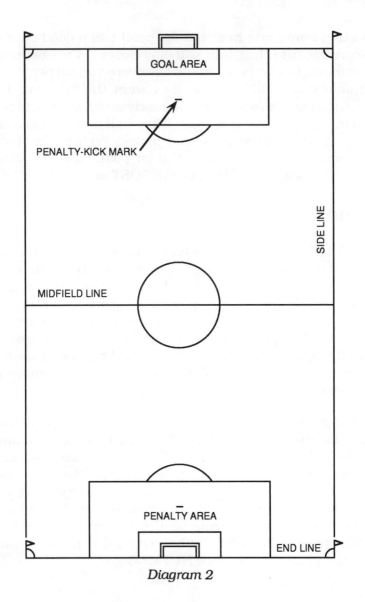

GOAL AREA

PENALTY-KICK MARK

SIDE LINE

MIDFIELD LINE

PENALTY AREA

END LINE

Diagram 2

boundary lines. (See CENTER CIRCLE, CORNER AREA, EIGHTEEN, ENDLINES, GOAL, GOAL AREA, MIDFIELD LINE, PENALTY AREA, PENALTY MARK, RULES and SIDELINES.)

FIELD VISION

The ability to see and know what is happening all around the soccer field.

 Field vision means that you are aware of where your teammates and the players on the other team are, where

"Field Vision"

the ball is, and where you are with respect to other players on the field. This knowledge is important whether or not you have the ball. Field vision helps you to understand the flow of play. It may give you or a teammate an offensive advantage or help you to get into a solid defensive position. (See TEAMWORK and "WATCH THE BALL".)

FIFA - FEDERATION INTERNATIONALE DE FOOTBALL ASSOCIATION

The international governing body of soccer. The responsibilities of FIFA include updating the rules of the game, promoting world soccer from amateur to professional levels and running the World Cup competition. FIFA was founded in 1904 by Belgium, France, Holland, Spain, Sweden and Switzerland. There are now over 178 member countries.

FOOTBALL

The international name for soccer. This name was first officially used in 1863 under the English title "Association Football."

FOOTBALL ASSOCIATION CUP

(See FA CUP.)

FORMATION

The way the player positions are arranged on the field. Formations are named with three numbers which stand for the number of fullbacks, halfbacks and forwards, in that order. Any formation will always include a goalie. For example, a 4-3-3 has a goalie, four fullbacks, three halfbacks and three forwards, and a 4-2-4 has a goalie, four fullbacks, two halfbacks and four forwards. The best formation for a team depends on the team's strength, speed, skill and need for a stronger offense or defense.

⚽ Formations must be based on the skills of the players on your team. Formations can be changed during the game. It is important that each player understand his or her role in the formation. (See POSITIONS.)

FORWARD

A player on the offensive line whose job is to score goals. Depending on the number of forwards in a formation, which is usually three to five, specific players may be called center forward, insides or wings.

A forward must be a fast runner. You should be a strong dribbler, header and shooter. Other tips: (1) always run to the ball - do not wait for the ball to come to you; (2) talk to your teammates; (3) move to an open space for a pass; (4) put pressure on the defense if you lose the ball to a player on the other team - because many times you can get the ball back under your control; (5) let the ball do the work; and (6) watch the ball at all times. (See CENTER FORWARD, FEINTING, INSIDE, LET THE BALL DO THE WORK, "WATCH THE BALL" and WING.)

"Foul"

FOUL

Breaking the rules of the game. The referee calls the fouls and the rules state what the penalty will be for each foul. Examples of fouls include: kicking, handling, charging, dangerous play and offsides. Fouls are called where and when they happen. It does not matter where the ball is or even if the ball is in play at the time the foul occurs. (See ADVANTAGE RULE and RULES.)

FOUR-FOUR-TWO (4-4-2)

A team formation which has a goalie, four fullbacks, four halfbacks and two forwards. Two of the fullbacks are usually in the sweeper/stopper positions. This formation gives a team a strong defense. (See STOPPER and SWEEPER.)

FOUR-THREE-THREE (4-3-3)

A team formation which has a goalie, four fullbacks, three halfbacks and three forwards. The outside fullbacks will frequently overlap to help the offense. (See OVERLAPPING.)

FOUR-TWO-FOUR (4-2-4)

A team formation with a goalie, four fullbacks, two halfbacks and four forwards. With the halfbacks playing offense and defense, this formation gives the team the equivalent of six offensive and six defensive players. Halfbacks should be strong and skilled because they must control the game.

FREE KICK

A kick made to put the ball into play. Except for kickoffs and goal kicks, the ball can be kicked in any direction. Players on the team without the ball must be at least 10 yards away from the ball until the ball is played. To be put in play, the ball must move at least the distance of one revolution. Free kicks can be either direct or indirect.

⚽ On offense, if you are the player who will kick the ball, you should look for teammates to whom you can make a pass. If you are on defense, you should mark a player on the other team. (See DIRECT FREE KICK, GOAL KICK, INDIRECT FREE KICK, KICKOFF and PENALTY KICK.)

FRONT TACKLE

A tackle used by a defensive player who is right in front of the player with the ball where the defensive player blocks the ball with his foot.

⚽ As you approach the player with the ball to make a front tackle, be sure that your weight is on your non-tackling foot (the foot which will not block the ball). (See Photo 7.) Lean forward towards the player with the ball and bring your tackling foot forward. Transfer your weight onto this foot

Photo 7   Photo 8

as you hit the ball. (See Photo 8.) Remember that you are trying to block the ball - not just kick it away. Be careful not to use your arms to push the other player or the referee may call a foul against you. (See TACKLING)

FRONT VOLLEY

A volley kick that can be used when the ball is right in front of a player and where the non-kicking foot stays on the ground.

⚽As you kick the ball, lean your upper body over the ball to keep the ball low, or lean back to send the ball high into the air. (See Photos 9 and 10). (See VOLLEY KICK.)

Photo 9   Photo 10

FULLBACK

A player on the defensive line, closest to the goalie, whose job is to keep the other team's offense from scoring and to move the ball up the field to teammates on the halfback and forward lines.

A fullback must be a very fast runner and should be a strong tackler and header. Other tips: (1) move to the ball - do not wait for the ball to come to you; (2) contain the player with the ball whenever you can; (3) if in doubt, kick the ball out to the sidelines; (4) look to the goalie for help; (5) stay between the ball and the goal when you are on defense; (6) talk to your teammates; (7) let the ball do the work; and (8) watch the ball at all times. (See CLEAR, CONTAINMENT, LET THE BALL DO THE WORK and "WATCH THE BALL".)

GIVE AND GO

(See WALL PASS.)

GOAL

1. One of two areas at opposite ends of the field which is 8 feet high and 8 yards wide. Each goal has two goal posts, a crossbar and a net.

2. A goal is scored when the ball passes all the way over the goal line between the goal posts and below the cross-

"Goal"

bar. (See CROSSBAR, FIELD, GOAL POST, INDOOR SOC-CER and NET.)

GOAL AREA

The rectangular area in front of each goal which measures 20 yards along the goal line (6 yards on each side of the goal) and 6 yards out into the field. Goal kicks are taken from the front of the goal area. The goal area is also referred to as the goal box. (See FIELD and GOAL KICK.)

GOAL BOX

(See GOAL AREA.)

GOALIE

A player whose job is to protect the goal. The goalie is the only player on the field who may use her hands to catch or throw the ball. However, the goalie may only use her hands to touch the ball inside the penalty area. The goalie may take up to four steps while holding the ball.

Good hands, quick reflexes and a strong jumping ability are required to be a successful goalie. Other tips: (1) get your body behind the ball and catch it as soon as you can; (2) if you cannot catch the ball, deflect it away from the goal; (3) when diving, be sure to cover up the ball; (4) narrow down the angle; (5) talk to your teammates; (6) distribute the ball quickly; and (7) watch the ball at all times. (See DISTRIBUTION, NARROWING THE ANGLE, PENALTY AREA and "WATCH THE BALL".)

GOALKEEPER

(See GOALIE.)

GOAL KICK

An indirect free kick given to the defensive team after the ball has gone out of bounds over the goal line and was last touched by a player on the offensive team. The ball is kicked from the goal area and must go out of the penalty area to be in play. No players from the other team can be inside the penalty area at the time of the kick.

⚽Unless you are a fullback or goalie who can kick the ball far, do not kick the ball down the center of the field. This is because a bad goal kick could be intercepted by a player on the other team who could take a shot on goal. The goal kick is the start of the offense so it should be kicked to a teammate. If the goalie will kick the ball, a fullback should cover the goal. The goalie can kick the ball up the field or the goalie can make a short pass to a fullback, at the side of the penalty area, who can dribble the ball up the field, pass the ball to another teammate or pass back to the goalie. A fullback could also make a goal kick to the goalie if the goalie is outside the penalty area. The goalie would then dribble the ball back into the goal area and pick it up. In general, all offensive players should move to be free for a pass. Players on the defensive team should mark the players on the offensive team and pay attention to when the ball is kicked. (See GOAL AREA, INDIRECT FREE KICK and PENALTY AREA.)

GOAL LINE

(See ENDLINES.)

GOAL POST

One of two posts which supports the crossbar and forms the sides of the goal. The goal posts must be tall enough so that the height of the goal, when measured from the bottom edge of the crossbar, is 8 feet. The inside edges of the goal posts must be 8 yards apart. The goal post may be made of metal or wood and the face of the goal post may be flat or rounded. (See CROSSBAR and GOAL.)

GUARD

(See MARKING.)

HALFBACK

A player who plays between the fullback and forward lines and whose job is to control the middle of the field. Half-backs play both offense and defense. Also referred to as midfielders, there are usually two to four halfbacks on the field for each team.

⚽Halfbacks must have good endurance and should be skilled at trapping, dribbling and passing. Other tips: (1) you should be in good offensive position to pass to the forward line and to back them up in case the forwards need to pass back to you, and you should also be in good defensive position to mark a player on the other team; (2) you may dribble the ball, but you should also look to pass to teammates who are open; (3) talk to your teammates; (4) move to open spaces to receive a pass; (5) move to the ball - do not wait for the ball to come to you; (6) let the ball do the work; and (7) watch the ball at all times. (See LET THE BALL DO THE WORK, MARKING, PASSING and "WATCH THE BALL".)

HALF-VOLLEY

A volley kick made just after the ball hits and bounces off the ground.

⚽The longer you wait to kick the ball after it bounces, the higher the ball will tend to go when it is kicked. (See VOLLEY KICK.)

HALFWAY LINE

(See MIDFIELD LINE.)

HAND BALL

A foul called when a player touches the ball with any part of the hand or arm (anywhere from the fingertips to the shoulder joint). This foul does not apply to a goalie within his own penalty area. The penalty for this foul is a direct free kick. Not all hand balls are punished. Some hand balls may not have been intentional or the player who touched the ball may not have gained an advantage by touching the ball. The referee decides whether or not to call a foul. Also, it is not a foul for a player to use his hands to make a throw-in or to place the ball on the ground before taking a free kick.

Photo 11

Photo 12

HANDLING

(See HAND BALL.)

HEADING

Using the head to pass, shoot or clear the ball.

⚽Keep your eyes on the ball. Make contact at the top of your forehead (near your hairline). Use your whole body, not just your neck, to propel the ball. (See Photos 11 and 12.) When practicing, throw the ball into the air a few inches above you and find the proper place on your head to head the ball. When this is comfortable, increase the height of your tosses. Later, set up a ball on a rope, like a tetherball, and practice jumping to head the ball. Have a friend toss the ball to you while you are kneeling. This teaches you the correct body and neck motion. If you are

"Holding"

on offense, you should try to make head passes to the feet of a teammate because it is easier for your teammate to control the pass. If you are heading the ball at the goal, a low head shot is harder for the goalie to stop than a head ball which is higher in the air. If you are on defense, clear head balls into the air and towards a sideline. (See BACKHEADING and DIVING HEADER.)

HOLDING

A foul called when a player uses her arms or hands to restrain or delay a player on the other team. The penalty for holding is a direct free kick. (See DIRECT FREE KICK.)

ILLEGAL CHARGE

(See CHARGE.)

INDIRECT FREE KICK

A free kick from which a goal cannot be scored unless the ball is first touched by at least one other player, from either team, after the kick. An indirect free kick is given to a team after the other team has made one of the fouls listed in INDIRECT FREE KICK FOULS. Kickoffs and goal kicks are also indirect free kicks.

⚽ If you are on offense and the kick is taken close to the goal, you should pass the ball to a teammate who is in a good position to take a shot on goal. Another idea is to shoot through the wall of defensive players, if there is a wall, and hope that the ball deflects into the goal. If you are on defense, make sure that you mark a player on the other team. Set up a wall if the kick is taken near your goal. Attack the ball when it is played. (See FREE KICK, GOAL KICK, INDIRECT FREE KICK FOULS, KICK OFF and WALL.)

INDIRECT FREE KICK FOULS

An indirect free kick is awarded for fouls such as: (1) illegal charge; (2) obstruction; (3) unsportspersonlike conduct; (4) dangerous play; (5) offsides; (6) interfering with the goalie; (7) improper substitution; (8) delay by the goalie in distributing the ball; (9) if the goalie carries the ball more than four steps; (10) if a player touches the ball a second time before another player touches it on a kickoff, throw-in or free kick; and (11) if the goalie touches the ball with his hands after the ball has been kicked to him by a teammate.

INDOOR SOCCER

The game of soccer played indoors. The rules of the game will vary from league to league. In most games, the ball is always in play because the players are allowed to play the ball off the walls. Professional indoor soccer is played on artificial turf. The two professional indoor leagues, the CISL and the NPSL, play on a field about the size of an ice hockey rink - about 200 feet long and 85 feet wide. Six players play on each team and substitutions may be made while the ball is in play. The game is 60 minutes long with four 15-minute periods. CISL goals are 7 feet 6 inches high and 14 feet wide, while NPSL goals are 8 feet high and 14 feet wide. There is no offsides foul. Other fouls are penalized by having the player who caused the foul sit in a penalty box for two to five minutes, depending on the foul. The team cannot substitute a player for the player in the penalty box. The team that has an extra player on the field is said to have a "Power Play." Penalty kicks are taken from a spot which is 24 feet in front of the goal. Certain severe fouls result in a Shoot-Out for the team that was fouled. In the CISL, all goals count as one point. In the NPSL, power play and shoot-out goals count as one point, penalty kick and regular goals count as two points and goals scored from over 50 feet away count as three points.

Because the indoor playing field is smaller than outdoor fields, you must change your playing style when you play indoor soccer. Because there is less room to dribble, you should make quick passes on offense. When you take a shot on goal, you should follow the shot because shots that miss may rebound from the walls near the goal and give you the chance to take more shots on goal. Also, when you have the ball, you can move past a player on the other team by playing the ball off the wall and back to yourself. Continual running is a major part of the game as there are quick changes from offense to defense. (See CISL, NPSL and SHOOT-OUT.)

INSIDE

A player on the forward line who plays in the center of the field, directly in front of the goal.

INSIDE OF THE FOOT KICK

When the ball is kicked with the arch-side of the foot between the heel and the knuckle of the big toe. This kick is used more for accuracy, such as for square passes, than for power.

⚽ Think of your foot as a golf putter which hits the ball.

Photo 13   *Photo 14*

43

You should point your toes to the side, with the inside of your foot facing front. Hit the ball in the middle (from top to bottom) in order to keep your pass low. (See Photos 13 and 14.)

INSIDE OF THE FOOT TRAP

When the inside of the foot is used to receive and control a ball coming on the ground or in the air at or below knee level.

⚽ The inside arch of your foot should face forward. Keep the foot with which you will trap the ball slightly off the ground and slightly ahead of your body to meet the ball. When the ball touches your foot, bring the foot back slowly. Keep your eyes on the ball and practice with both feet. An inside of the foot pass is easy to make after making this trap.

INSTEP KICK

When the top part of the foot, on the laces, is used to kick the ball.

Photo 15

Photo 16

⚽ The foot may be turned slightly outward so that the inside of the big toe connects with the ball. (See Photos 15 and 16.) This is a powerful and accurate kick which is used for passing, shooting and clearing. As with other types of kicks, the flight of the ball depends on the placement of the non-kicking foot, the lean of the body and where the ball is struck with the foot.

INSTEP TRAP

When the top of the foot, on the laces, is used to receive and control a ball below waist height.

⚽ Your weight should be on your non-trapping foot, with both knees slightly bent. Point the toe of the foot you will use to trap the ball at the ball and relax this foot when contact is made. Let your foot drop with the ball, slowing the speed your foot drops as it nears the ground. Practice with both feet.

INSWINGER

A kick where the ball curves in towards the goal. (See Diagram 3.) An inswinger usually comes from a corner kick or centering pass. (See BANANA KICK.)

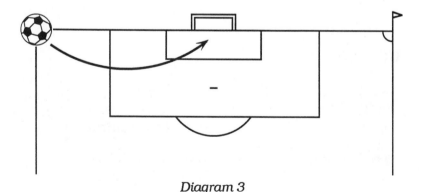

Diagram 3

45

INTERCEPTION

When a pass from a player on one team to a teammate is received by a player on the other team. Interceptions happen because the player on the other team hustles after the ball, the player expects that a pass will be made or, often, the player is lucky.

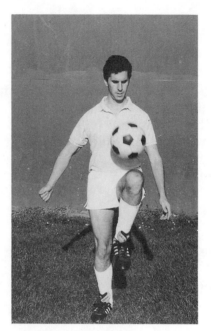

Photo 17

JUGGLING

Using the body, legs and head to keep the ball off the ground and under control as long as possible. Juggling is used to improve ball control and concentration.

⚽To begin juggling, use your feet to flick the ball into the air, or pick up the ball with your hands and drop it onto your foot or thigh. (See Photo 17.) When juggling, practice with specific parts of your body, such as your feet, thighs or head. When this is comfortable, switch the ball from one body area to another. Use both legs and vary the height and speed of juggling. For variety and increased skill, try juggling with a tennis ball. Juggling is only one way to improve your soccer skills, but developing this skill can prove very valuable in developing ball control. (See BALL CONTROL.)

JUMPING IN

A foul called on a player for leaving the ground and making unnecessary contact with a player on the other team. The penalty for this foul is a direct free kick.

⚽ When you jump up for a head ball and you are near players on the other team, be sure to jump up to the ball and not out at the players on the other team so that you are not called for jumping in. (See DIRECT FREE KICK.)

"Jumping In"

KEEPER

(See GOALIE.)

KICKING

1. To propel the ball with the feet in order to make a pass or shot.

2. A foul called when one player uses her feet to attempt to hurt or disrupt a player on the other team. The penalty for this foul is a direct free kick.

⚽ Tips for definition #1: Practice kicking with both feet. If you are alone, you can practice by kicking the ball against a wall. The position of your foot is important. To keep the ball low, keep the knee of the foot with which you will kick the ball over the ball. Your weight should be forward. Hit the ball in its center. Your non-kicking foot should be next to the ball. To send the ball high into the air, keep the kicking knee behind the ball. Your weight should be back. Hit the ball below center. Your non-kicking foot should be behind the ball. Practice kicking balls that are moving and balls that are still. When a ball comes from your left (right) and you want to one-time it, use your left (right) foot. If you try to kick with your right (left) foot, the ball might roll past you and you might make a bad kick. (See BANANA KICK, CHIP, DIRECT FREE KICK, INSIDE OF THE FOOT KICK, INSTEP KICK, ONE-TIME, OUTSIDE OF THE FOOT KICK and VOLLEY KICK.)

KICK OFF

The act of putting the ball into play at the start of each half, each overtime period and after all goals. The kickoff is made from the center circle on the midfield line. It is an indirect free kick. During a kickoff, two or more players on the offensive team may be inside the center circle, but no players from the other team may come into the circle until the ball has been touched by a player on the offense.

To be in play, the ball must roll forward at least the distance of one complete revolution. (See CENTER CIRCLE, INDIRECT FREE KICK and MIDFIELD LINE.)

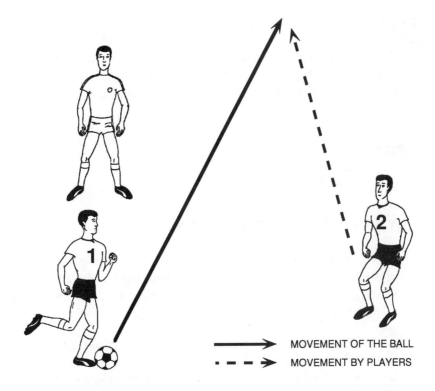

MOVEMENT OF THE BALL
MOVEMENT BY PLAYERS

Diagram 4

LAWS OF THE GAME

(See RULES.)

LEAD PASS

A pass to a space on the field to where a teammate is moving. (See Diagram 4.) The pass can be on the ground or in the air.

LEFT

Players on the forward, halfback and fullback lines who play on the left-hand side of the field when viewed from their own goal. (See FORWARD, FULLBACK and HALF-BACK.)

LEGAL CHARGE

(See CHARGE.)

LET THE BALL DO THE WORK

When a team makes passes from player to player, or to open space, in order to move the ball up the field and into scoring position, instead of having players dribble the ball all the way up the field.

⚽It is quicker and easier for a team to move the ball up the field with passes than it is for players to do the "work" themselves by running the length of the field with the ball. (See PASSING and OPEN SPACE.)

LINESPERSON

One of two officials who supervise the game from opposite sidelines. Linespersons are part of a three-person system - with the referee being the third person. Linespersons may call fouls, offsides and out of bounds, but their calls can be accepted or overruled by the referee. (See DUAL SYSTEM, REFEREE and THREE-PERSON SYSTEM.)

LINKMEN

Another name for the midfielder or halfback. (See HALF-BACK.)

LONG BALL

A style of soccer using long passes, such as crosses, long clears and lead passes. The ball moves greater distances, but is usually less controlled, than short ball. (See CLEAR, CROSSFIELD PASS, LEAD PASS and SHORT BALL.)

MAN-TO-MAN DEFENSE

A type of defense where every defensive player has a specific player on the other team to mark no matter where that player goes on offense. For example, if a right fullback guards the left wing, the right fullback would continue to

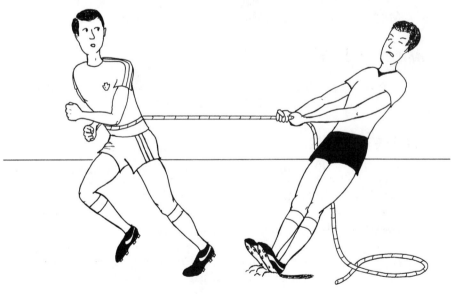

"Marking"

guard the left wing if the wing switched to the right side. (See MARKING and ZONE DEFENSE.)

MARKING

When a defensive player stays within playing distance of a player on the other team. This makes it difficult for the teammates of the player on the other team to pass to the player and keeps the defensive player in position to slow or stop the player on the other team if that player should receive the ball. Marking is also referred to as "guarding" or "covering" a player on the other team.

⚽ The distance you should be from a player to mark that player depends on where you and the player are on the field and your distance from the ball. The closer the player is to your goal or to the ball, the closer you should mark the player. This is because you will have less time and room to react if the player receives the ball. If your team is on defense, you should mark a player on the other team no matter what position you play. If you are on offense and are being marked by a player on the other team, try feinting in order to get free for a pass. (See FEINTING, MAN-TO-MAN DEFENSE and ZONE DEFENSE.)

MIDFIELDER

(See HALFBACK.)

MIDFIELD LINE

The line which divides the length of the field in half. (See FIELD.)

MISCONDUCT

A foul called when a player misbehaves. Unsportsperson-like behavior and violent conduct are two examples.

MSL - MAJOR SOCCER LEAGUE

A professional indoor soccer league in the United States. The league was founded in 1978 and was called the Major Indoor Soccer League. It received its present name in 1990. The league went out of business in 1992.

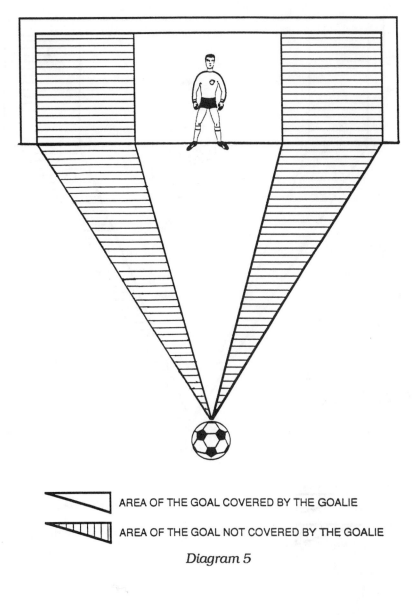

AREA OF THE GOAL COVERED BY THE GOALIE

AREA OF THE GOAL NOT COVERED BY THE GOALIE

Diagram 5

NARROWING THE ANGLE

When a goalie moves out of the goal towards a player on
the other team, who is going to take a shot on goal, in order
to reduce the open area of the goal at which the player on
the other team can shoot the ball. (See Diagrams 5 and 6.)

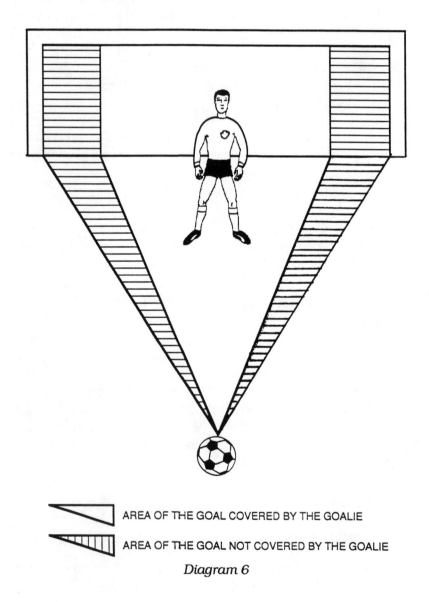

AREA OF THE GOAL COVERED BY THE GOALIE

AREA OF THE GOAL NOT COVERED BY THE GOALIE

Diagram 6

⚽The first rule for the goalie is "Do not hesitate." If you are the goalie, you must either stay in the goal and position yourself for a diving or jumping save or you must charge the player with the ball to make him rush his shot. If you do not make one of the two choices, you will not be in good position to stop the shot. If you do charge the player with the ball, make your charge after the player has passed all of your defenders. Remember that you only have to deflect the ball to prevent a goal. Be aware that a ball may be chipped over your head. You can tell if this will happen by the speed of the rolling ball and the time the player with the ball has to shoot. The faster the ball rolls and the less time a player has to shoot, the more difficult it is to make a good chip shot. You should also know how far you are away from the goal in case you block the shot and have to run back to the goal to make another save. (See GOALIE.)

NASL - NORTH AMERICAN SOCCER LEAGUE

A professional soccer league which was made up of teams from Canada and the United States. The league started in 1968 and went out of business in 1983.

NCAA - NATIONAL COLLEGIATE ATHLETIC ASSOCIATION

The governing body of college sports in the United States. It began in 1905 under the name of the Intercollegiate Athletic Association. In 1910, the association adopted its present name. In 1924, the Intercollegiate Soccer Association of America was formed under the direction of the NCAA and, in 1959, the National Collegiate Soccer Championship was first played.

NEAR POST

The goal post which is closest to the ball. (See Diagram 7.)

⚽The near post is important for the offense and the defense. On offense, the near post is closer to shoot at

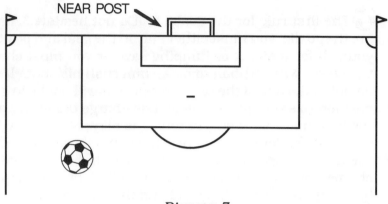

NEAR POST

Diagram 7

(although the goalie should be positioned closer to the near post than to the far post). An offensive player with the ball can draw the goalie towards the near post and then shoot at the far side of the goal or the player can cross the ball to a teammate who is at the far side of the goal. On defense, the near post must be guarded on corner kicks in order to block shots at the near post. A fullback usually has this job. The goalie must be positioned closer to the near side of the goal than to the far side of the goal. However, the goalie must also be ready to react quickly to a shot or pass to the far side of the goal. (See CORNER KICK, CROSSFIELD PASS, FAR POST and GOAL POST.)

NET

The mesh barrier which is attached to the crossbar and the two goal posts to make the goal. The net is usually pulled back from the goal and attached to the ground by stakes in order to give the goalie room to move in the goal. The net may be made of nylon, hemp or jute. (See CROSS-BAR, GOAL and GOAL POST.)

NPSL - NATIONAL PROFESSIONAL SOCCER LEAGUE

A professional indoor soccer league in the United States. The league was founded in 1984 and was called the American Indoor Soccer Association. The league received its present name in 1990.

NUMBER OF PLAYERS

Each team may have no more than eleven players on the field at any time during the game (although some youth leagues may allow a different number of players). There are no rules which say what positions the players may play, although only one player per team may play goalie.

NUTMEG

When the player with the ball dribbles or passes the ball between the legs of a defensive player. (See FEINTING.)

OBSTRUCTION

A foul called on a player who does not have the ball, or is not playing the ball, and who uses her body to block a player on the other team. The penalty for this foul is an indirect free kick. (See INDIRECT FREE KICK.)

OFFENSE

1. When a team or player controls the ball and tries to score a goal.

2. The "offensive" half of the soccer field is the half of the field where a team tries to score a goal. (See DEFENSE.)

OFFSIDES

A foul called on a player who is closer than the ball to the goal where his team is trying to score without at least two players on the other team being the same distance from, or closer to, the goal. The foul occurs at the time the ball is played. The penalty for this foul is an indirect free kick from the spot where the offsides took place. A player cannot be offsides on the player's defensive half of the field or if the ball is last touched by a player on the other team. There is no offsides foul on goal kicks, corner kicks, throw-ins or drop balls. If a player in an offsides position is not directly involved in the play and is not gaining an advantage for his team by being offsides, the referee has the option to allow play to continue. (See INDIRECT FREE KICK.)

ONE-ON-ONE (I on I)

When a player with the ball tries to dribble past a player on the other team.

⚽If you have the ball, make feints to move the defensive player who is marking you out of position and then dribble or shoot past the defender. If you are on defense, get in position and contain the player with the ball until your team gets back into position to support you. Tackle the player with the ball when you have a good chance to get the ball. (See CONTAINMENT, FEINTING, SHIELDING and TACKLE.)

ONE-TIME

When a player plays the ball as soon as it comes to her instead of receiving the ball, trapping it and passing off. One-time plays can be passes, clears, or shots on goal. This method of playing can be very effective because a team can move the ball quicker than it would if each player stopped the ball before making a pass or shot. However, one-timing requires a high level of skill to perfect.

⚽If you are on offense, you can make a one-time wall pass with a teammate to move the ball past a defender. A one-time shot on goal may catch the goalie out of position. If you are on defense, you should one-time clears near the goal if you do not have time to trap the ball because there are players from the other team near you. Whether you are on offense or defense, you should know where your teammates are before you make a one-time pass. (See CLEAR and WALL PASS.)

ONE-TOUCH

(See ONE-TIME.)

ONE-TWO

(See WALL PASS.)

ONE-WHISTLE SYSTEM

A system of refereeing where play is stopped after the referee blows the whistle, but can be restarted without a second whistle. On corner and goal kicks, the referee may simply give an arm signal for play to begin again. This system is used in FIFA games. (See FIFA and TWO - WHISTLE SYSTEM.)

OPEN

A player who is free to receive the ball. An open player is one who is not marked by a player on the other team. (See MARKING.)

OPEN SPACE

Areas of the field where there are no players.

⚽Open space is very important in terms of ball and player movement. If we "let the ball do the work," passes made to open areas, where teammates can run to meet the ball, spread the defense out and allow more room for offensive movement. (See LET THE BALL DO THE WORK.)

OPPONENT

A player on the other team.

OUT OF BOUNDS

When the ball leaves the field of play by going completely over the sidelines or endlines. A ball can be out of bounds on the ground or in the air. The ball is not out of bounds if it rebounds from a goal post or hits a corner flag and stays on the field. An out of bounds ball is considered a dead ball. The method of restarting play will depend on where the ball went out of bounds. If the ball went over the sidelines, play is restarted with a throw-in. If the ball went over the endlines, play is restarted with a goal kick or corner kick, depending on which team last touched the ball before it went out of bounds. (See CORNER KICK, DEAD BALL, ENDLINES, GOAL KICK, SIDELINES and THROW-IN.)

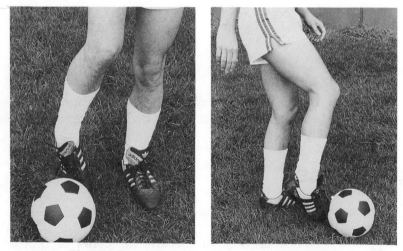

Photo 18   *Photo 19*

OUTSIDE OF THE FOOT KICK

When the ball is kicked with the kicking foot pointed down and the toes turned in toward the other foot. The ball is struck on the outside part of the laces.

⚽ This kick is not as powerful as other kicks. However, it can be a very deceptive kick in passing or shooting because the ball will tend to curve in the air. (See Photos 18 and 19.)

OUTSIDE OF THE FOOT TRAP

When the outside of the foot is used as a wedge to receive and control ground balls or balls falling in front of a player.

⚽ The foot you will use to trap the ball should be in front of you and your weight should be on your back foot. Place the outside of your foot over the ball as it hits the ground. Practice with both feet. A good fake can be used with this trap. If the ball is coming from the right, pretend you will run with it to the left. Just before it gets to you, put your weight on the left foot. Then, lean towards the ball with your right foot receiving the ball and dribble to the right.

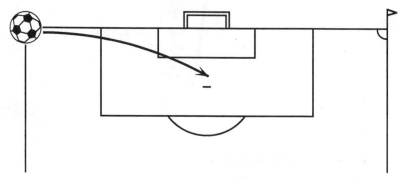

Diagram 8

OUTSWINGER

A kick where the ball curves away from the goal. (See Diagram 8.) An outswinger usually comes from a corner kick or centering pass.

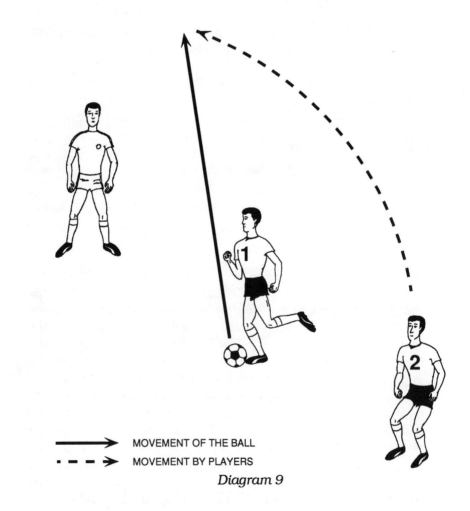An outswinger keeps the ball away from the goalie and so it is used as a pass to set up a shot on goal by a teammate. (See BANANA KICK.)

MOVEMENT OF THE BALL
- - - ➤ MOVEMENT BY PLAYERS

Diagram 9

OVERHEAD VOLLEY

A volley kick which is used to clear or shoot the ball behind a player and which is made with both feet off the ground. This is also known as a bicycle kick.

⚽Keep your eyes on the ball. Swing your non-kicking foot first. As the top section of your body falls backward, swing your kicking foot up to meet the ball. Land on your back with your arms out to the side to cushion your fall. To keep the kick low, you must start your kick early so that you hit the ball at the height of your jump. This kick should only be practiced when a qualified supervisor is present and you should first practice this kick on a mattress.

OVERLAPPING

When an offensive player without the ball moves past a teammate with the ball to an area in front of the teammate with the ball. (See Diagram 9.) The player who overlaps may or may not receive the ball, but that player becomes an additional offensive player who the other team must try to cover. The most frequent overlaps occur when a fullback overlaps a halfback or a halfback overlaps a forward. In some cases, fullbacks will overlap all the way up the field to a wing position.

⚽Communication between teammates is very important. If you are the player who overlaps, you should let your teammate with the ball know that you are free to receive a pass. Also, because you have left your regular position, it is important to let your other teammates know that there is a gap in your team's defensive coverage. Someone on your team must cover your position if the other team gets the ball. Finally, because overlapping spreads out the defense, it is better for the player who overlaps to run on the outside of the player with the ball (closer to the sidelines). If you are on defense, you should contain the player with the ball and let your teammates know that the player on the other team who is overlapping needs to be marked. (See CONTAINMENT, COVER and MARK.)

OVERTIME

The extra period of play used to decide the winner of the game when the score is tied at the end of regulation play. The rules for overtime play vary from one soccer association to another. FIFA rules use overtime only during tournaments. One 15-minute sudden-death period is used. If no goal is scored, a second 15-minute sudden-death period is used. If no goal is scored in the second period, each team takes five penalty kicks. The team which scores the most goals wins. The APSL uses two 7-1/2-minute sudden death periods. If there is no winner, each team takes five penalty kicks. The NCAA plays two 10-minute periods. These periods are not sudden-death. Non-tournament games are allowed to end in a tie. In tournament games, the tie is broken by penalty kicks. (See PENALTY KICK and SUDDEN-DEATH.)

OWN GOAL

A goal accidently scored by a team against itself. This may happen when a goalie drops the ball into the goal, when a fullback makes a misguided kick or head ball which goes into the goal or when a back pass to the goalie is missed by the goalie. No matter how the goal happens, the other team gets a point for the goal.

Because soccer is a low scoring game, these goals can often be the deciding factor in a game. DON'T GIVE UP if an own goal is scored by your team. Talk with your teammates about what went wrong, try to correct the mistake and then get on with the game.

PASSING

The act of giving the ball to a teammate. The ball can be passed in the air or on the ground. It can be kicked, headed or propelled to a teammate by using other parts of the body.

⚽If you are on offense, let the ball work for you - don't dribble if you can make a pass to a teammate who is in a better position. Teammates who do not have the ball should move to open spaces where they can receive a pass. Always move to the ball - don't wait for the ball to come to you. Use both feet to pass. It is wise to vary the type of passes made, such as mixing long balls with short balls and wall passes with crossing passes. If you are on defense, do not be afraid to pass the ball back to the goalie if you do not have anywhere else to pass the ball. The same holds true for forwards who can pass back to midfielders and midfielders who can pass back to fullbacks. (See BACK PASS, CENTER PASS, CROSSFIELD PASS, LEAD PASS, LET THE BALL DO THE WORK, OPEN SPACE, SQUARE PASS, THROUGH PASS and WALL PASS.)

PENALTY

(See FOUL.)

PENALTY AREA

The rectangular area in front of each goal which measures 44 yards along the goal line (18 yards from each goal post) and 18 yards out into the field. The goalie may use his hands in the penalty area. All fouls committed in the penalty area which require direct kicks against the defending team will result in penalty kicks. (See DIRECT KICK, EIGHTEEN, FIELD and PENALTY KICK.)

PENALTY KICK

A direct free kick awarded to a team which has had a foul committed against it inside the other team's penalty area and the penalty for the foul is a direct free kick. The penalty kick is made by one player from the penalty mark which is 12 yards out from the goal. The goalie must stand on the goal line and cannot move until the ball is played. All other players must stand outside the penalty area (at least 10 yards away) until the ball is played. The player who will kick the ball may only touch the ball once. The ball must be touched by another player before the kicker can play the ball again. This rule applies to rebounds from the goal post or crossbar.

⚽If you are taking the penalty kick, you should make a hard, accurate shot. It is best to shoot at the lower corners of the goal because this is the hardest type of shot to stop. On defense, the goalie should be on her toes and ready to leap. The goalie should try to sense where the kicker will place the ball and jump to that side. This can be done by watching where the kicking foot connects with the ball. It is hard to stop a well-placed penalty kick, but a goalie may be lucky. All other players, whether on offense or defense, should be ready for a rebound. (See DIRECT FREE KICK, PENALTY AREA and PENALTY MARK.)

PENALTY MARK

The line from where penalty kicks are taken. The penalty mark is 12 yards out in front of the goal and is 2 feet long. (See FIELD and PENALTY KICK.)

"PLAY ON"

A call by the referee to indicate that she has seen a foul but has decided to let play continue. (See ADVANTAGE RULE.)

POSITIONS

The general area on the field where a player plays and the player's duties in that area. The main positions are: goalkeeper, fullback, halfback and forward. There is always one goalie but the number of other positions varies with the formation used. However, each team can never have more than eleven players on the field. Each position requires an all-round ability with special skills. "Total Soccer" allows players to leave their regular positions to move to other positions on the field. (See FORMATION, FORWARD, FULLBACK, GOALIE, HALFBACK and TOTAL SOCCER.)

PRACTICE

Repeating an activity to improve and perfect the activity.

⚽ The more often you practice an activity and the more correctly you practice that activity, the better you will be at that activity. Practice helps you to improve as a soccer player. You can practice ball control, kicking, trapping, dribbling and running. Team practice helps the team work together. Teams can practice offense, defense and group skills. Practice, for both the individual player and the team, can be made more enjoyable by varying drills or adding competition to the practice. When working with a soccer ball, it is important that you practice with both feet. (See EXERCISE and WARMUP.)

PUNCHING

1. A way the goalie stops a shot on goal from scoring by hitting the ball away from the goal with one or two fists. A goalie will punch the ball when a shot is too high or too hard to catch, or if there are too many players from the other team near the goalie for the goalie to be sure of catching the ball.

2. A foul called when one player hits a player on the other team with a fist or hand. The penalty for this foul is a direct free kick.

⚽ Tips for Definition #1: You should try to use both hands to punch the ball. This will help you make good contact with the ball. You should hit the ball with the flat part of your fist (not directly on the knuckles), and should punch the ball away from the goal. (See DIRECT FREE KICK, DIVING and SAVE.)

PUNTING

A way a goalie kicks the ball by dropping the ball and kicking it before it reaches the ground. A punt usually sends the ball farther than a drop kick or a throw.

⚽It is important to keep your eyes on the ball while punting. You should extend your arms and drop (not throw) the ball to your kicking foot. Your kicking foot should be brought up to meet the ball and extended with a strong follow-through after contact with the ball is made. This helps to increase the distance of the kick. The goalie should try to direct the punt to a teammate. (See DISTRI-BUTION.)

PUSHING

A foul called when one player uses his hands or arms to shove or move a player on the other team. The penalty for this foul is a direct free kick.

⚽When you jump up for head balls or make a shoulder tackle, be sure to keep your arms down at your side so that you are not called for pushing. (See DIRECT FREE KICK.)

RED CARD

A card which the referee holds up to show that a player has been ejected from the game. (See EJECTION and YELLOW CARD.)

REFEREE

The person who supervises the game. Referees are responsible for deciding disputes and enforcing the rules of the game. They have the power to stop the game, call fouls, warn players or coaches, and eject players or coaches from the game. There are two types of referee systems: the dual system and the three-person system. The system used in a game will depend on which soccer organization's rules are in use.

⚽Referees are human and may make mistakes. Complaining to or about the referee does not help. All players should respect the referee's decision. (See DUAL SYSTEM, EJECTION, LINESPERSON, THREE-PERSON SYSTEM and WARNING.)

RIGHT

Players on the forward, halfback and fullback lines who play on the right-hand side of the field, when viewed from their own goal. (See FORWARD, FULLBACK and HALF-BACK.)

RULES

The official rules of the game of soccer. The rules were created by the English Football Association in 1863 and have been changed many times since then. FIFA rules, the international rules, serve as the model for the rules used by most professional soccer leagues. The NCAA college rules and the rules used by the National Federation of State High School Associations are based on FIFA rules. FIFA's "Laws of the Game" are listed in seventeen sections which range from the length and width of the field and the size of the ball to scoring, fouls and referees. FIFA allows modifications of certain of its rules for soccer games played by women or players under 16 years of age. Indoor soccer leagues may have different rules.

⚽Whether you are a referee, a soccer player or a fan, knowing and understanding the rules of the game will help you to better enjoy the game of soccer. Rules make the game work for everyone - players and fans alike. (See FIFA.)

RUNNING

Moving the legs quickly in order to cover as much distance as possible in the shortest amount of time.

⚽ Soccer is a game of motion. If you do not run, you will soon find yourself out of the play, if not out of the game. If you are on offense, quickness to the ball may help you beat a defender and score a goal. If you are on defense, quickness to the ball may put you in a position to save a goal. If you are in good shape, you will be able to play a better game. All positions run fast and for long times. Halfbacks tend to cover the most distance, while fullbacks and forwards tend to sprint more. Goalies should run too. Long distance runs are good for your endurance, while short sprints will help you to develop quickness.

RUNNING TIME

The length of time which has passed in a soccer game. (See TIME OUT.)

SALT AND PEPPER BALL

Another name for a black and white soccer ball. (See SOCCER BALL.)

SAVE

Stopping a goal from being scored. Saves are usually made by the goalkeeper who catches the ball, punches it away or deflects it out of bounds. Other defenders can make saves by blocking shots on goal with their bodies or heading or kicking a shot away. (See DIVING and PUNCHING.)

SCISSORS KICK

A volley kick used to send the ball forward and which is made with both feet off the ground.

70

⚽A scissors kick requires perfect timing, but is a powerful kick if done right. The non-kicking foot is swung first and then the kicking foot makes contact with the ball. To keep the ball low, lean forward over the ball as you kick. To send the ball high into the air, lean back as you kick. (See VOLLEY KICK.)

SCORE

1. The number of goals each team makes in a game. The team with the highest score wins the game.

2. To make a goal. A team receives one point for every goal no matter how the goal is scored or whether the goal is scored during normal play or by a penalty kick.

SCOREBOOK

The book in which the official record of a soccer game is kept. Entries in a scorebook include the score of the game, team lineups, the names of the players who score goals, the time of each goal and penalties.

SCOREKEEPER

The person who puts information into the official scorebook.

SCORER

1. The person who makes a goal.

2. Another name for the scorekeeper.

SCREENING

(See SHIELDING.)

SELLING A DUMMY

When a player with the ball makes a feint which causes a player on the other team to move in a direction away from the ball while the player with the ball passes or dribbles in a different direction. Selling a dummy can also be done by an offensive player who does not have the ball. For example, a halfback runs to meet a pass coming to her. If a player on the other team is close by, he will probably follow her. However, if he is watching the halfback and not the ball, he might follow her as she lets the ball continue through her legs to a teammate.

To make sure that the play works, it is important that teammates talk to each other or know where they are on the field in relation to each other. If you are the person making the feint, you must check to see that a teammate is near you, or will be near you, when the feint is made. Otherwise, the other team may get the ball. If you are the person who will receive the ball, you should let your teammate making the feint know that you are open to receive the ball. If you are the defender, you should mark your player while you continue to watch the ball. (See FEINTING.)

SHIELDING

When a player with the ball protects the ball from a player on the other team by keeping his body between the ball and the player on the other team.

It is easiest to shield the ball by dribbling the ball with the outside of your foot which is farthest from the player on the other team. This way, it is possible to make a pass or, by hiding the ball from your opponent's sight, make a feint and then dribble in another direction. (See FEINTING.)

SHOOTING

Using the body, usually the feet or head, to direct and propel the ball at the goal.

⚽An accurate shot has a better chance of scoring a goal than a powerful, but inaccurate, shot. The closer you are to the goal to shoot, the better is your chance of scoring. Although goals can be scored from outside of the penalty area, it is probably better to pass the ball to a teammate who may be in a better position to shoot. The best shots are low ones because it is easier for a goalie to jump for a high ball than it is for the goalie to dive for a low ball. This means that you should concentrate on leaning over the ball when shooting. When practicing shots, it is best to kick a moving ball (instead of a still ball) because kicking a moving ball is more like what happens in an actual game. Learn to shoot with both feet.

SHOOT-OUT

1. In the CISL and NPSL, a free kick awarded to a team which has been fouled and the penalty for the foul is a shoot-out. A player from the team which was fouled starts 50 feet away from the goal and must score a goal within five seconds. Only the goalie and the player with the ball can be on the field. The player with the ball may touch the ball as many times as he likes, within the five second limit, and may play the ball off the goalie, the walls and the glass.

2. A method used to break ties in the NASL after the end of the overtime periods which involved five players from each team taking alternate kicks in order to score a goal. Each player would start 35 yards out from the goal and would have to score a goal within five seconds.

⚽If you are the player with the ball, you must act quickly because of the five second time limit. It is helpful to have a specific strategy in mind. You have three major choices: (1) to shoot from outside, which gives you the best angle;

(2) to dribble in and try to beat the goalie; or (3) to chip the ball over the goalie's head if the goalie comes out from the goal. In indoor soccer, you could also play the ball off the wall to yourself. If you are the goalie, you may either run at the ball to narrow the angle and try to stop the shot, or fake a run and hope that the shooter makes a poor shot. (See CHIP, CISL, INDOOR SOCCER, NARROWING THE ANGLE, NASL and NPSL.)

SHORT BALL

A style of soccer using short passes, such as triangles and wall passes. The ball moves shorter distances, but is usually better controlled, than long ball. (See LONG BALL, TRIANGLE and WALL PASS.)

Photo 20

Photo 21

SHOULDER TACKLE

A tackle used by a defensive player who is at the side of or in front of the player on the other team with the ball, where the defensive player uses her shoulder to knock the player with the ball away from the ball.

⚽ The tackle is nonviolent. If you are the person making the tackle, you must go after the ball and not the player with the ball. Be sure to keep your arms at your sides so that a pushing foul is not called against you. (See Photos 20 and 21.) (See TACKLING.)

SIDELINES

The boundary lines which mark the sides of the soccer field. The length of the sideline is the same as the length of the field. FIFA requires a minimum length of 100 yards and a maximum length of 130 yards. NCAA rules set the length between 110 and 120 yards. (See FIELD.)

Photo 22

Photo 23

SIDE VOLLEY

A volley kick used for balls coming at a player between ankle and waist height where the kicking leg is raised to the side and the non-kicking foot is on the ground. The ball is kicked with the instep of the foot.

⚽ Practice a side volley by throwing a ball into the air and kicking it. Point your toe for instep kicks. The further forward you lean your body, the lower the ball will go. (See Photos 22 and 23.) (See INSTEP KICK and VOLLEY KICK.)

SLIDE TACKLE

A tackle used by a defensive player who is on the side of, or slightly behind, the player with the ball, where the defensive player slides on the ground with one leg extended to knock the ball away.

⚽ You should tackle with your leg farthest from the player with the ball. Time the tackle so that you can hit the ball

Photo 24   Photo 25

when the player with the ball has the leg nearest to you away from the ball. Point the toe of your tackling leg for extra reach. (See Photos 24 and 25.) Practice tackling on your right and left sides. When you are making a tackle, be careful to hit the ball and not the player. It is a tripping foul if you hit the player with the ball before you hit the ball. This could result in a penalty kick if the trip happens inside the penalty box. However, it is not a tripping foul if you hit the ball first - even if the player with the ball falls down. Also, since an improper slide tackle could injure you and the player with the ball, slide tackles should only be used as a last resort - such as to stop a breakaway. (See TACKLING.)

SOCCER

The name given in the United States to the game known in the rest of the world as football. (See FOOTBALL.)

SOCCER ASSOCIATION FOR YOUTH (SAY)

Also known as SAY Soccer U.S.A., this organization was founded in 1966 to promote soccer for children between the ages of six and eighteen.

SOCCER BALL

The round object which must be played into the goal to score points and win the soccer game. The ball is usually made of leather, although some leagues allow rubber balls. There are many types and sizes of soccer balls. The official ball must have a circumference of 27 - 28 inches and must weigh between 14-16 ounces. Soccer balls come in many colors, but the most common colors are black and white. These are also known as "Salt and Pepper Balls." Most soccer balls used in the United States have 32 panels while most European soccer balls have 16 panels.

The official soccer ball is a size 5 ball. Players over the age of twelve should use this ball. Players between the

Photo 26

ages of six and eleven years should use a size 4 ball. Those players under the age of six should use a size 3 ball. Practicing with a smaller sized ball will often help to improve a player's soccer skills.

SOLE TRAP

When the bottom of the foot is used as a wedge to receive and control ground balls or balls falling in front of a player.

The leg you will use to trap the ball should be bent slightly at the knee and your weight should be on your non-trapping foot. (See Photo 26.) Practice with both feet.

"SQUARE"

A call made by a player to a teammate with the ball which tells the teammate with the ball that the player is alongside in case the teammate needs to make a pass. (See SQUARE PASS.)

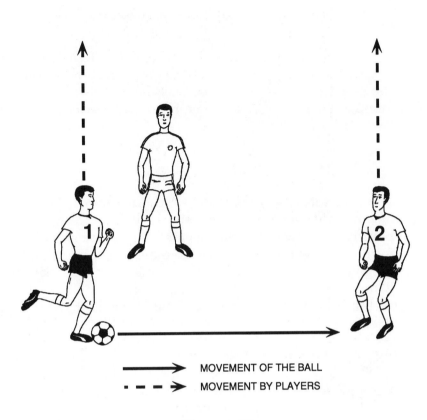

| → | MOVEMENT OF THE BALL |
| - - - → | MOVEMENT BY PLAYERS |

Diagram 10

SQUARE PASS

A sideways pass to a teammate who is on either side of the player with the ball. The player without the ball is usually about 5 to 15 yards away from the teammate with the ball. (See Diagram 10.)

⚽ If you are the player without the ball, you should let your teammate with the ball know that you are open to receive a pass. A square pass is easiest to control if it is made on the ground. (See "SQUARE".)

STOPPER

A defensive position in a formation with four fullbacks (including the stopper) where the stopper plays in front of the goal and between the fullback and halfback lines. A stopper position is used together with a sweeper. (See SWEEPER.)

STRATEGY

The plan for the soccer game. Although soccer is a game of constant motion, some aspects of the game can be planned before the game begins. These include: team formations, what positions each player will play and plans for goal kicks, corner kicks, throw-ins and free kicks. The game plan may be specific, such as playing the ball to a certain player, or general, such as playing short or long passes.

A good team plan will take into account the strengths and weaknesses of your team and your opponent's team. Each player can also have his own strategies, such as the way he might dribble in a one-on-one situation, or the way he might shoot the ball against a certain goalie. (See FORMATION, POSITION, TEAMWORK and THINKING.)

STRIKER

(See FORWARD.)

STRIKING

A foul called when one player uses her hands or arms to hit or try to hit a player on the other team. The penalty for striking is a direct free kick. (See DIRECT FREE KICK.)

SUBSTITUTION

When a player on the field is replaced by a player from the same team who is not on the field. The substitute player should report to the referee when coming onto the field. FIFA rules allow substitutions after a goal has been scored or on a goal kick or corner kick. The rules in other leagues may allow substitutions on throw-ins. The number of substitutions allowed in a game will also depend on the rules of the league. FIFA allows two substitutions per game in official competition and five substitutions per game in other matches, while high school rules allow any number of substitutions.

⚽ If you are not playing in the game, you should be "warmed up" and ready to go into the game at any time.

SUDDEN DEATH

When, during an overtime period, the game ends as soon as a goal is scored. (See OVERTIME.)

SWEEPER

A defensive position in a formation with four fullbacks (including the sweeper) where the sweeper plays in front of the goal and behind the fullback line. The sweeper is the last defensive player in front of the goalie. It is the sweeper's job to clear any balls and to mark any player on the other team who gets through the defense. A sweeper position is used together with a stopper.

⚽ If you are the sweeper, you must be careful not to drop too far back into the goal area. You should move up to pull the players on the other team offsides. (See STOPPER.)

SWITCH

When two players on the same team change positions with each other.

⚽ When teammates switch, each player should know the area of the field for which he is responsible and which player on the other team he must mark.

TACKLING

Using the feet and body to take the ball away from a player on the other team.

⚽Tackle when you have a good chance to get the ball - usually just after the player with the ball touches it. Another good time to make a tackle is when the player with the ball has just received the ball and is trying to get it under control. Unless you are making a slide tackle, you should never reach out with one foot at the ball. This is because you will be off-balance and the player with the ball will be able to dribble past you. Instead, take small steps at the ball. This helps you keep your balance and position in front of the player with the ball. (See FRONT TACKLE, SHOULDER TACKLE and SLIDE TACKLE.)

TEAMMATE

A player on the same team.

TEAMWORK

The work and cooperation of all eleven teammates on the field. Teamwork is one of the most important parts of soccer. No one player can do everything. Every player must rely on the passes, defense and support, both physical and mental, of her teammates.

THIGH TRAP

When the top or side of the thigh is used to receive and control the ball.

⚽Raise the knee of the leg you will use to trap the ball with your leg bent down at the knee. Lower your knee as the ball makes contact. The ball should hit the fleshy part of your thigh, not the knee. Practice with both feet. Many players make volley passes after this trap because the ball is brought under control above the ground. (See VOLLEY.)

82

THINKING

When a player uses his brain to add to and improve his soccer abilities.

⚽Thinking is a soccer skill and can be the reason why two players with equal ball skills may play very differently. Thinking differs from strategy in that thinking is done on a personal level while strategy is done on a team level. You must think about where your teammates are when you have the ball and where they may run to receive a pass. You need to know where the ball is at all times and where you should be when you do not have the ball. Knowing when you should contain or challenge a player on the other team and when you should dribble or pass the ball are also the results of thinking. (See STRATEGY.)

THREADING THE NEEDLE

When one player makes a pass to a teammate where the ball goes between two players on the other team and it does not look like there would be room to make the pass.

THREE-PERSON SYSTEM (3-PERSON SYSTEM)

A system where one referee and two linespersons supervise the game. The referee has full authority over the game, makes all calls, is the official timekeeper and has the power to penalize all fouls made by players or coaches. The referee works with two linespersons who may make calls, although their calls may be overruled by the referee who has the final decision. (See DUAL SYSTEM, LINESPERSON and REFEREE.)

THREE-THREE-FOUR (3-3-4)

A team formation with a goalie, three fullbacks, three halfbacks and four forwards.

THROUGH PASS

A pass which is made between two defensive players to a teammate and which moves the ball closer to the goal. (See Diagram 11.)

⚽ The area on the field to where you are passing the ball will determine the speed and accuracy needed for the pass. If the area is open, you can lead your teammates with a slow, easy to handle pass. If the area is crowded with defensive players, then a faster and more accurate pass is needed. When you are close to the goal and the defense is strong, keep the ball on the ground. This makes it easier for your teammates to receive and control the ball. Your teammates may make another pass or a one-time shot on

⟶	MOVEMENT OF THE BALL
∎ ⎯ ⎯ ➤	MOVEMENT BY PLAYERS

Diagram 11

the goal. Communication with your teammates is also very important. Tell one another when you are ready to make a pass or are open to receive a pass. Talking with your teammates will also help you avoid being caught offsides. (See LEAD PASS, OFFSIDES and ONE-TIME.)

THROW-IN

Using the hands to throw the ball back into play after it has gone out of bounds over the sidelines and was last touched by a player on the other team. This is the only time during the game when a player other than a goalie may use her hands. Only one throw is allowed. The other team gets the ball if the throw-in is not legal. The ball can be thrown in any direction, but a goal cannot be scored directly from a throw-in.

⚽Hold the ball equally with both hands and bring it behind your head. Throw the ball straight from behind and over your head. (See Photo 27.) Both feet must touch

Photo 27   *Photo 28*

the ground, so, if you take a step, be sure to drag the toe of your back foot along the ground. (See Photo 28.) Do not cross the sideline until the throw has been made. Throw-ins can be of value to the offense if done well. A throw-in should go to your teammate's feet because it is easier to trap or pass the ball right from the throw. Fake the throw a few times to fool the defense. If you are on your defensive half of the field, you should remember that you can throw the ball to the goalie. One way to help you increase the distance you can throw the ball is to practice throw-ins with a basketball. This is because it is heavier than a soccer ball.

TIMEKEEPER

The person who keeps track of playing time. The time-keeper starts and stops the clock at times stated in the rules or ordered by the referee. The referee may also serve as the official timekeeper. (See RUNNING TIME and TIME OUT.)

TIME OUT

When the clock stops. The referee may order a time out when she warns or ejects a player, or when a player is injured. If the referee is not the official timekeeper, she will signal the timekeeper to stop the clock. Time-outs last as long as the referee feels is necessary. Play will restart with a drop ball, if neither team had control of the ball, or with a free kick, if a foul had been made before the time out. (See DROP BALL, FREE KICK, RUNNING TIME and TIMEKEEPER.)

TOE

To kick the ball with the point of the foot.

⚽Unless you are reaching to kick the ball, such as to make a clear or to shoot on goal, you should not use the toe to kick the ball. This is because you have little control over where the ball will go when it is hit with the toe.

TOTAL SOCCER

A system of play where all team members play both offense and defense. Total soccer is based on the idea that, because soccer is a game of constant motion, any player may find himself anywhere on the field. This is because players overlap and switch positions. A "total soccer" player understands all aspects of the game and has the ability to play all positions on the field. The total soccer system was made famous by the Dutch during the 1974 World Cup finals between Holland and West Germany. (See OVERLAPPING and SWITCH.)

TOUCHLINE

(See SIDELINES.)

TRAPPING

The act of receiving the ball in the air or on the ground and bringing it under control. A trap can be made with various parts of the body and all traps involve using the body as a cushion.

⚽ Relax that part of your body which you will use to make contact with the ball - as if you were using that part of your body to catch an egg. The ball does not have to be stopped dead, only brought under control. Practice throwing or kicking balls against a wall and then trap the balls. Learn to use both feet to trap and learn to trap the ball from all sides and angles. Keep your eye on the ball. Move to the ball if the ball seems too high or is falling in front of you. If you wait for the ball, a player on the other team may get to it first. (See CHEST TRAP, INSIDE OF THE FOOT TRAP, INSTEP TRAP, OUTSIDE OF THE FOOT TRAP, SOLE TRAP and THIGH TRAP.)

TRIANGLE

An offensive formation with three players which is used to pass the ball around an opponent or to kill time. (See Diagrams 12 and 13.)

MOVEMENT OF THE BALL

- - -> MOVEMENT BY PLAYERS

Diagram 12

If you are on offense and you do not have the ball, you should move to the open side of your teammate, with the ball, to give your teammate the chance to make a pass. Using triangles to pass the ball can be very effective in moving the ball up the field. Communication between teammates is always important. If you are on defense, you should play in front of, but slightly away from, the player with the ball.

MOVEMENT OF THE BALL
MOVEMENT BY PLAYERS

Diagram 13

TRIPPING

A foul called when one player uses her legs to cause a player on the other team to fall. The penalty for this foul is a direct free kick. An accidental trip may be punished by the referee if the player who made the trip gained an advantage.

⚽Be careful that you do not trip a player on the other team when you are trying to make a slide tackle. If the foul is called in the penalty area, the other team will be given a penalty kick. (See DIRECT FREE KICK.)

TURNOVER

When one team loses control of the ball to the other team. This can happen when the ball goes out of bounds, when a foul is called, when a pass is intercepted, when a player on one team loses the ball to a player on the other team or dribbles or passes the ball out of bounds, or when a steal results from a tackle. Goalie saves do not count as turnovers because the offensive team has finished the play by taking a shot on goal.

TWO-WHISTLE SYSTEM

A system of refereeing where play is stopped after the referee blows the whistle and the ball is dead until the referee blows the whistle a second time. For example, when a whistle is blown for offsides, the defending team cannot take the free kick until the second whistle. The two-whistle system slows the pace of the game, but makes it easier for the referee to maintain control. This system is used mainly in high school and non-FIFA games. (See DEAD BALL and ONE-WHISTLE SYSTEM.)

UNIFORM

(See EQUIPMENT.)

UNITED STATES SOCCER FEDERATION

(See USSF.)

UNSPORTSPERSONLIKE CONDUCT

A foul called when a player's behavior is unacceptable under the rules of the game. Examples include: repeated breaking of the rules and such fouls as verbal abuse or physical signals to another player or referee. The penalty for this foul is an indirect free kick. FIFA rules call this foul "Ungentlemanly Conduct." (See INDIRECT FREE KICK.)

USISL - UNITED STATES INTERREGIONAL SOCCER LEAGUE

A soccer league formed in 1993 where professional and amateur teams compete indoors and outdoors.

USSF - UNITED STATES SOCCER FEDERATION

The organization which governs soccer in the United States. The USSF was founded in 1912 under the name of the American Amateur Football Association. This association was named as the U.S. representative to FIFA one year later. The USSF received its present name in 1974 when it was known as the United States Soccer Football Association.

USYSA - UNITED STATES YOUTH SOCCER ASSOCIATION

The youth division of the USSF. This organization was founded in 1974 and promotes soccer for young people.

VIOLATION

(See FOUL.)

VIOLENT CHARGE

(See CHARGE.)

VIOLENT CONDUCT

A foul called for actions such as fighting or abuse toward the referee or another player. The penalty for this foul is a direct free kick. If the conduct is violent, the player could be warned or ejected from the game by the referee. (See DIRECT FREE KICK, EJECTION and WARNING.)

VOLLEY KICK

A type of kick where the ball is played while it is in the air. It can be a one-time kick or it can be played from a trap. A volley can be used to pass, clear or shoot the ball.

⚽Keep your eyes on the ball. Timing is important. To make a high kick, lean back while kicking. For a low kick,

"Wall"

lean over the ball while kicking. (See FRONT VOLLEY, HALF VOLLEY, ONE-TIME, OVERHEAD VOLLEY, SCIS-SORS KICK and SIDE VOLLEY.)

WALL

When two or more defenders stand shoulder to shoulder in order to protect the goal when the other team is given a free kick within scoring distance. The wall cuts down the shooter's angle at the goal.

⚽A wall should be set up 10 yards from the ball and should be positioned between the ball and the goal. The closer to the goal the kick is taken, the more defensive players should be part of the wall in order to protect the goal. If you are on offense and you are going to take the kick, you may shoot directly at the goal by curving the ball around the wall or by chipping the ball over the goalie's head. You can also pass to a teammate who may be open for a shot. On defense, the goalie should tell the players on the wall where to stand so that the goal is covered. If you are part of the wall, you should line up quickly in case the wall has to move. Keep your arms at your sides or in front of you. It is not a hand ball if the ball hits your arm and referee decides that you did not mean to hit the ball with your arm. Defensive players who are not on the wall should mark players on the other team.

WALL PASS

A pass where one player receives the ball and quickly returns it to, or in front of, the teammate who made the pass - as if the ball had been played against a wall. (See Diagram 14.) Wall passes are used to move the ball around a player on the other team who is in front of the player with the ball.

⚽ Communication between teammates is important. If you are the player who makes the pass, you should move past the player on the other team after you make the pass.

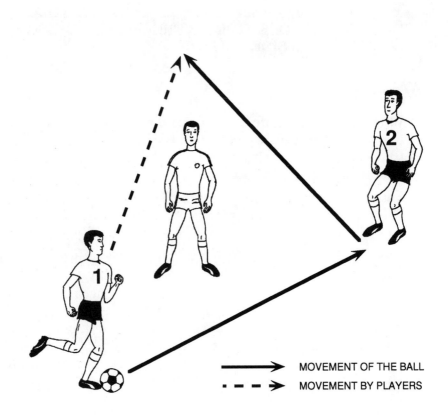

MOVEMENT OF THE BALL

- - - ➤ MOVEMENT BY PLAYERS

Diagram 14

The return pass should be a lead pass. The play works best when the pass is on the ground. (See LEAD PASS.)

WARMUP

Physical exercise before a game or practice. The warmup prepares the body and mind for what is to come. It should include slow stretching exercises to loosen muscles and a slow run to help the circulation. A warmup helps the player to relax and minimize injuries.

⚽ You should make sure that all parts of your body are loose and warmed up before you begin hard exercise. (See EXERCISE and PRACTICE.)

WARNING

When the referee tells a player or coach, who may be on or off the playing field, that the player or coach may be ejected from the game if his behavior does not improve. A warning is given to a person who continually breaks the rules, who argues with the referee, commits a foul on purpose or tries to hurt another player. Most warnings are given for the action of one player against a player on the other team. Play is restarted with the type of free kick that the rules set for the foul. To signal a warning, the referee holds up a yellow card.

⚽ Repeated fouls after a warning will cause the player's ejection from the game. If you receive a warning, you should take your warning quietly and courteously. You will not help your team if you argue and are ejected. (See EJECTION, FREE KICK, RED CARD and YELLOW CARD.)

"WATCH THE BALL"

A phrase yelled by coaches and players on the soccer field (and often found in soccer books) which means: "Pay attention to what is going on!" If a player does not know where the ball is, then that player is not fully involved in the game.

WING

A forward who plays near the sidelines. Wings can shoot on goal, but they usually bring the ball down the field and make centering passes to the inside forwards. Most teams use two wings.

⚽ Speed and passing skills are required. Other tips: (1) stay wide near the sidelines for passes from your fullbacks or halfbacks and run to the ball when it is passed; (2) when dribbling, keep near the sidelines to spread out the defense; (3) look for the chance to make good passes; (4) talk to your teammates; and (5) watch the ball at all times. (See CENTER PASS.)

"Watch The Ball"

"WITH YOU"

A call made by a player to a teammate, with the ball, to tell the teammate that the player is close and can help if the teammate needs someone to pass to. The player without the ball can be alongside or behind the teammate with the ball.

WORLD CUP

The world championship of professional soccer - a tournament among the national teams of the FIFA countries. The finals are played every four years with regional qualifying competition beginning two years before. Twenty-two finalists are invited from their regions. The host team and the defending champion also play. In the finals, the twenty-four teams are divided into six groups of four. The teams play a round-robin tournament where each team plays every other team in their group. The top two teams in each group are put into four groups of three. The four group winners play single elimination games to determine the winner. World Cup competition was started by FIFA in 1928 and the finals were first played in Uruguay in 1930. (See FIFA.)

YELLOW CARD

A card which the referee holds up to show that the referee has warned a player and that the player may be ejected from the game if the player continues to break the rules. (See EJECTION, RED CARD and WARNING.)

ZONE DEFENSE

A type of defense in which every defensive player guards a specific area of the field. The defensive player should mark any player on the other team who comes into that area. For example, the right fullback might be assigned the zone from the middle of the goal to the right sideline and from the goal line to near the midfield line. The zone will vary from coach to coach. The boundaries of the zones often change during the game. (See MAN-TO-MAN DEFENSE.)

About The Author

Paul S. Delson has played, coached and refereed competitive soccer for over twenty years. Paul lives in San Francisco, California, and practices law in his spare time.

MAIL ORDER FORM

Please send _____ copies of **SOCCER SENSE: TERMS, TIPS & TECHNIQUES.** I understand that I may return the books for a full refund of the purchase price if I am not satisfied. Please deliver the books to:

Name: _____

Address: _____

_____

_____

Books:
($9.95 each) $_____

Sales Tax:
(Please add $0.82 for
each book shipped to
California addresses) $_____

Shipping:
($2.25 for the first
book and 50¢ for each
additional book) $_____

TOTAL $_____

Please send a check or money order in the total amount to:

Excalibur Press
4 Chestnut Street, Suite 100
San Carlos, CA 94070

Please allow 4-6 weeks for delivery.

Volume discounts are available. Please write Excalibur Press for details.